Julian Sturgis

A Book of Song

Julian Sturgis

A Book of Song

ISBN/EAN: 9783337006747

Printed in Europe, USA, Canada, Australia, Japan

Cover: Foto ©Thomas Meinert / pixelio.de

More available books at **www.hansebooks.com**

A BOOK OF SONG

BY

JULIAN STURGIS

LONDON

LONGMANS, GREEN, AND CO.

AND NEW YORK : 15 EAST 16ᵗʰ STREET

1894

PREFACE

I MUST not send out this little book without a line
of thanks to Messrs. BLACKWOOD for their per-
mission to print again some twenty of these songs
which were first published in their Magazine many
years ago. And, seeing that in courtesy I must
write this, perhaps I may be pardoned for adding
a few words more, to this effect indeed—that I
have made songs all my life at happy moments
when the mood was mine. The first—which, how-
ever, is not to be read here—I wrote down with a
pencil borrowed from the nurse who was assisting
me to bed (I can dimly recall the surprise and
pride and joy) ; the last was made but the other
day. It is, of course, open to the critic, if by
chance they meet for a moment his glancing eye,
to remark that all alike are childish, and so pass

on to a more worthy prey. But since I have been drawn into these brief confessions, this little show of egoism, I should like to say, too, that no song in this little book was made for music, an art which I love, like a savage or a babe, with a consummate ignorance ; yet there are many which I have sung to myself in strict solitude, all on one note. I must have known, I think, some of the joy of the real singer who can both ease his heart and keep the tune. And this may be said, too —that, had I made choice from my songs in my undergraduate days, when some of these were written, I should have admitted more of a complexion sad as night ; for in those singing days of the reed voice 'twixt man and boy the subtlest, saddest pleasure may be drawn from converse now and then with our good comrade Melancholy. Together we take the road, and in these mornings of our wayfaring a face once seen in the passing crowd, or the mere amorous air of fleeting Spring, may set us throbbing with a song of love.

CONTENTS

A

BOOK OF SONG

—•◦•—

SONG

If I might ride on puissant wing
  The realms of air,
What joy were in the journeying,
  Wert thou not there?

From star to little star I'd go
  To seek for thee,
Till e'en the clouds that hold the snow
  Would weep for me.

WESTERLY

ALL night the west wind bowed the ships at sea,
All night the west wind bent the forest tree,
    But now with night the rain has passed away ;
And now her hand is glossy as fine silk,
And now, with throat as white and soft as milk,
    All westerly my darling's like the day.

·The burnished pigeons feed beneath the beech ,
    The pastures all athirst have drunk their fill ;
A stillness holds the world more full than speech,
    And with the waiting world my heart is still.

Would I were silk about my darling's wrist !
Would I were air her parted lips that kissed,
Or locket of old-fashioned amethyst
        To rest at her sweet will !

STRAY NYMPH OF DIAN

I WENT a-hunting with Queen Dian's maids ;
　　Our sandals, bright with dew,
Swept through the grass, and down the listening
　　　glades ;
　　Our hounds beside us flew ;
On swept the chase, but I stood gazing there,
Poor wounded doe beside a thorn-tree fair.

For there, with fallen blossoms on his head
　　I spied the sleeping boy ;
The chase had left me breath, but now it fled
　　For pain of too great joy ;
I panted so, the thong, that crossed my breast
And held my quiver, hurt me where it pressed.

I could not tell if he did smile or frown
　　For shadow's fickle play
On brow and cheek, and on his lip like down
　　A loving shadow lay,
And there I set my lips—ah, joy and woe !
For now no more a-hunting may I go.

A PAGEANT OF THE AIR

THE sailor boy sings out on the ruffled blue,
 The sea bird turns in the air all silver white,
A breath of heaven makes the world anew
   For man's delight.

Like trumpet tones, when angel onset rings,
 The great clouds move from the west, all sailing
 free,
The fluting breeze in the tight cordage sings
   Of ships at sea.

To find her beauty in the cloud and wave
 My wakened soul goes forth, I know not why,
And earth is fair, and heaven is strong to save,
   And glad am I.

THROUGH THE IVORY GATE

I HAD a dream last night,
  Dream of a friend that is dead ;
He came with dawn's first light
  And stood beside my bed :

And as he there did stand,
  With gesture fine and fair,
He passed a wan white hand
  Over my tumbled hair,

Saying : ' No friendship dieth
  With death of any day,
No true friendship lieth
  Cold with lifeless clay.

Though our boyhood's playtime
  Be gone with summer's breath,
No friendship fades with May-time,
  No friendship dies with death.'

Then answer had I made,
   But that the rapture deep
Did hold me, half afraid
   To mar that rose of sleep.

So with closed eyes I lay,
   Lord of the vision fair ;
But when 'twas perfect day,
   Only the day was there.

A GREEK GIRL

SOMEWHERE have I seen her wander
Bearing bay and oleander,
And the soft air murmured round her
   With a delicate sweet motion ;
And from far there followed after,
Ringing laughter, mocking laughter,
Inextinguishable laughter,
Of the merry girls who found her
   Singing by the purple ocean
Songs I made for her adorning
In the pleasant time of morning.

AGATHON

AWAY with me to Athens, Agathon!
  There let us stand in idle mood to see
  Great Phidias' pupils shape the marble fair,
Till perfect forms by art from chaos won,
        And garments fine and free
  Stand cool and clearly lined in violet air,
Statues and workmen in such beauty clad,
We cannot pause to judge, but are divinely glad.

Bright Agathon, again I challenge thee!
  The shade has reached the wrestlers; 'tis the
      time
  For merry play and contest. Hark! with sound
Of laughter rippling, pausing daintily,
        What shouts of welcome chime!
  Young Charmides, methinks, doth take the
      ground,
Or naked Lysis, fresh from eager game,
Draws down the strigil light o'er breast and limbs
    aflame.

There let us lie and listen too, for know
   I spied but now amid the olive trees
That strange old face we loved a while ago.
          Aye, it was Socrates,
Or else a satyr, by some god's gift wise,
Leered through the close gray leaves to mock our
    dazzled eyes.

Oh that glad eve at supper, when by me
   He lay and talked, till I was wild with joy
Of thinking quick new thoughts, nor cared to see
   The dancing girl from Corinth, nor the boy
Who bore the wine-jar to us—and 'twas good
To see thee lie and laugh at my unwonted mood.

O Agathon, and how we burned that day,
   With Æschylus' great chorus in our ears,
To see our queenly vessels far below
Ride down and dash to foam the quiet bay,
   And thine eyes turned to mine were bright with
    tears,
          And all thy face aglow,
For the old bard who fought at Marathon,
And that our sires were brave when Salamis was
   won !

O friend of mine, call back our friendship's dawn,
  The day I reined my horse on yon steep road
Where the long pageant moved in order meet,
        And boys from lowland lawn
Moved upward to the shrine with fragrant load,
  And 'mid all voices thy voice sang so sweet,
That its clear beauty touched my soul like pain,
And many deemed, I wis, Harmodius come again.

      Vain, vain, the hope is vain :
Our skies are drear, and through the ragged firs
  A slow cold wind is moaning.   Far away
        From driving clouds and rain
A vocal breeze the blue Ægean stirs,
  And o'er its dimpling plain quick sea-birds play ;
But no Queen Athens in her beauty bare
Bathes, warm with golden light, in the clear violet air.

The city of the pleasant gods is cold ;
  No more the mellow sunlight streams
On naked rocks that spring to marble rare ;
        Temples and legends old
  Are vacant as a poet's vanished dreams,
And, though we know the dawn was wondrous fair,
Yet by no charm of art nor labour slow
Can we bring back the light that died so long ago.

My Agathon, we cannot strive with Time ;
  The shadows steal around us, and afar
Grows in our ears the moan of ocean gray :
            Weak hand nor weaker rhyme
  Can charm again that spirit like a star
That rose awhile o'er Hellas.   Stay, oh, stay,
Dear friend !   I cannot bear the days to be.
Ah, Hermes, give him back !   Must he too fade
    from me ?

GRAPES

COME, boy Bacchus, a bunch of grapes—
    The bunch you dearest treasure!
'Twill fill my soul with exquisite shapes,
    For well I know the pleasure
Of a rich ripe grape slow pressed i' the mouth—
Bringing me dreams of the lusty South,
Of sun-brown youth and sun-bright maiden,
And all a-laughing, and all a-laden
    With grapes, grapes, grapes beyond all measure!

A ROSEBUD

GIVE me a rosebud, Rosebud-lips,
  Only a rosebud sweet as the giver,
Fresh as the swallow's joy who dips
  A slanting wing in the flowing river,
Fresh as the dawn and dewy wild,
Rosebud gift of a rosebud child.

AN APPLE

HERE, little Apple-face, bring me an apple
Bright as your baby cheek!
Let old grave men with an old world grapple;
But you be merry, merry and meek,
Glad as a little careless Greek,
And like this apple clean and crisp—
Oh! how I love your baby lisp,
And—thank you for the apple!

HALF GREEK

HALF Greek adown a Highland glen,
  And singing to the open sky,
I passed beyond the ways of men,
  And found my vale in Arcady.

The bees were drowsy on the slope,
  The air was, like enchantment, still ;
And all my heart beat high with hope
  Of wonders on the Grecian hill.

The light cloak from my shoulders flew,
  My bare brown limbs were light and free ;
The lark, whose rapture thrilled me through,
  Was but a singing bird to me :

For I was Greek in Hellas' prime,
  And all the world was young and fair,
And Greek the bees that robbed the thyme
  And Greek the charm that held the air.

Ah no ! not Greek these Highland hills
  That melt in blue to misty sky,
Nor Greek nor glad these hurrying rills
  That sing no songs of Arcady.

From tree to tree the whisper creeps :
  ' Look, sister, at the wayward man !
His are the eyes of one who sleeps
  Within the vale Arcadian.'

' Hush, hush,' the pine-tree sighs, ' and look ! '
  The lav'rock peeps from heather sweet,
And headlong leaps the Highland brook
  To break in laughter at my feet.

AN UNEQUAL GAME

A MOMENT of loving and laughter,
  A glance and a gay good-bye ;
If you one short week after
  Forget, then why not I ?

To you but a moment's feeling,
  A touch and a tender tone—
A wound too deep for healing
  To me who am left alone—

A wound and an aching wonder
  That lightly you go from me,
That we must be kept asunder
  By the cold abiding sea.

MY FAULT

MINE was the fault, I asked too much of thee—
The deeps of love, the heights of constancy.
Thy blue eyes, loving laughter, loving love,
From friend to friend, pleasure to pleasure rove,
And glancing now below and now above thee,
Challenge the world, the whole bright world, to
    love thee.

Mine was the fault, I asked too much of thee—
The brook to yield its bright variety,
The skylark of the world to drop for rest
To the poor shelter of one lonely breast.
I thought to form thee to my nicest measure,
And make thee wise and good for mine own
    pleasure.

C

Aye, mine the fault ; but now, since here I fall
Low on my knees in thy confessional,
O frolic saint, forgive me !   Not for me
Is fellowship in thy gay company ;
But if one hour thou weary of their play,
Lean on my heart that hour and make my day.

TO ALTHÆA SINGING

Now am I jealous of things musical,
       And would instruct mine ear
In the deep silence of the world to hear
       The withered leaf down fall,
And the far pebble shifted on the shore ;
       And I would learn the lore
Of babbling rivulets and bubbling springs,
The multitudinous murmur of the grass,
And notes of all the little birds that pass
Till air is rhythmical with pulsing wings :—
       But soft ! My mistress sings ;
           I ask no more.
Enough for me to list her lightest tone ;
I hear all music hearing her alone.

WHENCE ?

WILL he come to us out of the West
  With hair all blowing free ?
Will he come, the last and best,
  Over the flowing sea,
  Prophet of days to be ?

Aye, he will come ; the unseen choir
  Attend his steps with song,
And on his breast a deep-toned lyre,
And on his lips a word like fire
  To burn the ancient wrong.

Bay-crowned and goodlier than a king,
  With voice both strong and sweet
The song of freedom he will sing,
And I from out the crowd shall fling
  My rose-wreath at his feet.

BOY'S SONG OF HOPE

Is morning near?
Look out, old watchman, from your towered
    height—
Look to the eastern hills! Is there not light?
        The clouds of woe and fear,
            Are they not drifting?
        Morning is here, is here,
            And night is lifting.

Is morning near?
Old man, thine eyes are dim ; give place to me!
I say the light is up for all to see.
        The golden day draws near,
            And clouds are drifting ;
        The day, the day is here,
            And night is lifting.

Break forth and sing,
Hills that leap heavenward for the first sunbeams,
Close pastures, hanging woods, and clear bright
    streams

Where cows stand knee-deep, fields of fair increase,
Where men may toil in hope and rest in peace !
  Wealth is a little thing
   When clouds are drifting,
  When dawn is on the wing
   And night is lifting.

  Make great your song,
All men, all women toiling on God's earth ;
Though ye be weak, your work of little worth,
  Though ye have waited long
   While clouds were drifting,
  Look up, forget your wrong,
  Look up, and lift your song,
   For night is lifting.

  Lift up your gates,
Ye cities that have lain in woe and sin,
Lift up your gates for light to enter in !
  The King of glory waits
   While clouds are drifting ;
  Lift up your golden gates,
   For night is lifting.

Who is the King of glory?   Look afar!
Comes he a warrior from triumphal war?
Ah no!   In country lane and city street,
Men shall look up and feel the sunshine sweet
   Grow round them and increase,
    While clouds are drifting.
   Who comes our Prince of peace
    When night is lifting?

    Eastward we gaze;
The gates of morning, like the opening rose,
Blush with his coming; light grows large and clear;
    Black night and fear
    With host of shadowy foes
    Fly forth before his rays
     Like clouds adrifting.
    Who comes to rule our days
     When night is lifting?

A MOMENT AND FAREWELL

O BIRD, flying far to the ocean,
   O bird, flying far to the sea,
I ask for one buoyant emotion,
   One thrill of thy rapture for me.

In the height of the heights were it given,
   For a moment to hang like a star,
To see and to know as in heaven,
   With sorrow and trouble afar—

To pause in the fulness of being,
   On wings that are spread for my flight,
To see without trouble of seeing,
   And to hie me away to the night.

LOOKING BACKWARD

O MY child love, my love of long ago,
  How great was life when thou and I were young!
The world was boundless, for we did not know,
  And life a poem, for we had not sung.

Now is the world grown small, and we thereon
  Fill with mere care and toil each narrow day;
Elves from the wood, dreams from my heart are
    gone,
  And heaven is bare, for God is far away.

Canst thou not come and touch my hand again,
  And I look on thee with grave innocent eyes?
Thy God has many angels; I would fain
  Woo for one hour one angel from the skies.

O my child love, come back, come back to me,
  And, laughing, lead me from the toil and din!
Lay on my heart those small hands tenderly
  And lovingly to let the whole world in.

A CALL TO BATHE

LEAP naked from the sunlight warm
  Down to the cool and clear,
And thou shalt rise, and in thine arm
  Thy vanished boyhood bear.

The dust of travel done away,
  And rags of worn romance,
Again shalt thou affront the day
  With joyful countenance :

And glad as he who ran aflame
  By the Greek river's brim,
Ere the great eagle's shadow came
  And darkling stooped to him.

SPRING SONG

A BABY joy is awake in my heart,
  And flutters his wings in song;
For now the wintry winds depart,
  And summer days are long.

The woods that late were cold and bare
  With jocund babble ring;
Slides on slant fans adown the air
  A bird too glad to sing.

O buoyant air! O joyous air!
  You wake the weary throng,
And rhythmical with music rare,
And filled with sunshine everywhere,
  You touch our lips to song.

A SONG OF LONDON SPRING

THE twigs in the sooty gardens
   Are touched with a tender green,
And I think 'tis the prettiest Springtide
   That ever yet was seen.

The face at the old club window
   Forgets to scowl as I pass,
And out in the park the children
   Roll all in the cool green grass.

Last night a new shower from heaven
   Washed all the old world clean,
And I think 'tis the prettiest Springtide
   That ever yet was seen.

SLEEP

BEAUTIFUL up from the deeps of the solemn sea
Cometh sweet sleep to me,
From silent cool green deeps,
Where no one wakes and weeps,
   Cometh, as one who dreameth,
With slowly waving hands,
   And the sound of her garment seemeth
Like waves on the level sands ;
      So cometh Sleep.
There is rest for all mankind,
When her slow wings stir the wind ;
With lullaby the drowsy waters creep
To kiss the feet of Sleep.

JOY OF THE SWIMMER

HE is glad as a bird on still wings driven
    By a wind that follows free ;
Above him the sun in the height of the heaven,
    Beneath him the cool green deeps of the sea.

He bends his neck in the clear salt water,
    He spreads his arms to the far bright sun ;
He dreams a dream of a sea king's daughter,
    Wayward and hardly won.

In cave of the sea a mermaid singing,
    A siren voice from an island fair,
Out in the tide the seaweed swinging,
    Bird song in the air.

O salt of the sea, O joy of the swimmer's heart,
How dear thou art !

THE ELF-KING'S YOUNGEST DAUGHTER

DOWN the new-born brooklet dancing,
Through the dappled shadows glancing,
Foam about her white feet creaming,
All her wayward hair out-streaming,
Laughing on the laughing water,
Dances down the Elf-king's daughter,
  Youngest daughter fair ;
All the trees would bend toward her,
All the rocks be strong to guard her,
All the swaying rushes whisper,
And the little grasses lisp her
  Praises everywhere.

Close around the warm air lingers
Lovingly, the while her fingers
With a modest upward gesture
Seem to draw a shade for vesture
  Of her loveliness :
Though, meseems, she moves so purely,
Sliding on her path demurely,

Gazing with clear eyes serenely,
She were clad not half so queenly
    In a royal dress.

Now adown the stream she's sweeping ;
Now she stays and looks afearing,
O'er the ledge of granite peering,
Sees the headlong torrent leaping,
Sees far down the sullen boulders,
While the long locks round her shoulders
        Gather tenderly.
Now with little laugh atremble
All her shrinking to dissemble,
Flashing through the rainbow shower,
With her white feet launched below her,
And her hair drawn high above her,
Swift as lady to her lover
        Down the fall goes she.

Now, when quiet night has clouded
All the river broad and stately,
Down the stream she moves sedately,
In her soft hair warmly shrouded,
        Lulled by melody.

Prone between the dark trees' sighing,
Listening to the wheat replying,
Dreaming on the dreaming water,
Floats the Elf-king's youngest daughter
    To the dreaming sea.

EVENING AT HURLINGHAM

LIKE jewels dull the Chinese lanterns shine,
  Looped on the bosom of the fragrant night ;
    Music like drowsy wine
      Wooes to delight ;
    Musing or murmuring low,
    The men and women come and go
      From dark to sight.

    Low the Orient lanterns gleam
      With dim rich light,
    Dreaming a luxurious dream
      In our Western night ;
While in the blue most pure and deep
    Moon doth her vigil keep,
And above music murmur and the glow ·
    Of lamps hung low
Shines, as a beacon light beyond the foam,
The star of hope—the star of home.

OFF ISKANDERÛN

'TIS May, my love, on the Southern sea,
  And the night comes softly on,
And the moon shines fair, as never to me
  A moon of the Northland shone :

And oh but my heart is beating, love,
  With a passionate dream of thee,
And my lips of themselves repeating, love,
  The name that is dear to me !

O moon in the mantle of ragged cloud
  That ridest the Northern night,
Breathe low to my love in her London crowd
  Of the South and its dear delight :

Breathe low to my love how the Southern moon
  Leans down to the passionate sea ;
Breathe low to my love how the South winds
    swoon
  On the breast of the passionate sea.

IN COLORADO

I DREAM of the dance and the gallant show,
    Ball-room lights and a scented air,
Where ladies softly ebb and flow,
    Silken tide on a marble stair,
Lilies and ladies as lilies white
Swaying and playing for my delight.

Now is the whisper heard again,
    Breathed at the ear in the flying dance,
Now I recover the fine disdain
    That hurt my heart in a careless glance ;
A thousand thousand miles away
I see and I hear these ladies gay.

The keen air creeps through the wall of logs,
    And brings me a dream that is light as air ;
I sleep on the floor with the men and dogs,
    And dream of a lady that's debonair ;
Where feet of the dancers come and go,
She smiles on a man that I used to know.

All of a row the snow peaks gleam,
   Diamond stars of the Western night ;
With diamond stars from out my dream
   These ladies pass as coldly bright,
For morning has come, and the hinds begin
To go to their labour till eve close in.

IT IS TIME

O LOVE, dear love, must I weep in a lonely room ?
    O heart, dear heart, is there never a throb for
        me ?
Spring flowers enow in meadow and hedgerow
        bloom,
    And a slow soft light creeps over the sombre
        sea.
            It is time for the goddess to wake—
                Aphrodite, Aphrodite !
            It is time to arise from the foam.
                Awake, awake,
            And go to my darling's home !

O born of the sea, step light on thy rosy feet
    When night is still and there's never a one to
        hear ;
Stand where her window glints in the desolate
        street,
    And murmur alow to my love that her lover is
        near.

It is time for my darling to wake—
    Aphrodite, Aphrodite !
It is time for my darling to love.
    Awake, awake,
And tell her I die for love !

O love, my love, what will I not dare for thee ?
  Shall I dive deep down in the pitiless sea for a
    gem ?
Shall I bring the tiger's skin for a girl in glee
  To sweep, as she dances by, with her garment's
    hem ?
      I am mad for a girl's gray eyes—
        Aphrodite, Aphrodite !
      It is time to awake from the foam.
        Awake, arise,
      And go to my darling's home !

STREET MUSIC

THE song rings out a wild wild passionate song—
  O love, my love, I spread my wings and away ;
Over the sea on wide wide wings and strong
  I fly to the land of my love, to the light of day,
To my Italy—Italy, O sweet land to me,
I speed on the wings of a song far over the
    sounding sea.

Mad music peals and rings in my passionate heart ;
  My heart is afire for love and the sweet sad
      smile
Of a musing girl who listens with lips apart,
  And wills me away to kneel at her feet awhile.
O pale slight girl, my desolate heart to thee
Flies hot with a passionate song far over the wild
    white sea.

I am coming, my girl; I come to the city of flowers
    fair,
    To sing with a tremulous voice that thou art
        more sweet than they—
More white than the lily pale on the pale clear
    violet air,
    More sweet than the red red rose that faints at
        the close of day ;
I am coming with song and love, with spring and
    the violet bloom,
I am coming to find thine eyes like stars in the
    ilex gloom.

AT THE OPERA

HER woman's heart was given,
    False heart for a ruby true ;
Her eyes were made of heaven
    And sold for the sapphire's blue.

Diamonds are on the finger
    Where lips have pressed full fond ;
Where loving eyes would linger,
    Collar of diamond.

The old jewel-monger chuckles
    At the gifts of my lord the earl,
And he bows to my lady's buckles
    And her Garagantua pearl.

But her box the poet passes
    With a sigh for love astray,
And he turns from her opera-glasses
    To the farce that the players play.

A LONDON SONG

My lady's the lily of ladyhood,
  And when she has passed the stair
The trebled scent of an April wood
  Is sweet on the troubled air.

For her be vagrant verse of mine
  But a wedding of house and land,
And, wheresoever she hap to dine,
  A seat at her host's right hand.

For her be dozen-of-button gloves
  And dozens of sweet champagne ;
But never the least of all the loves
  Will come at her call again.

A BEATING HEART

O EYES of a dreaming maiden,
  O voice of a singing bird,
How comes the soul in your music
  Whereby our souls are stirred ?

There's love in your shy soft glances,
  There's love on your singing lips ;
When you play on the grand piano
  There's love in your finger tips.

But under the fair white bosom,
  With a kerchief drawn across,
A little machine is ticking
  To reckon profit and loss.

TO AN INTERESTING PERSON

GIRL, whose grave enchanted eyes
    Look a thousand miles away,
Ne'er shalt thou, so seeming-wise,
    Love as simpler maidens may.

Thine are fancies roving fair,
    Islands of the Southern seas,
Thine to breathe the unknown air
    Of the lost Hesperides.

Thee the siren voices sing,
    Thee Medusa smiled upon ;
Thou hast seen the flashing wing
    High in heaven, Bellerophon.

Yet perchance some summer morn
    Thou shalt wake, and waking sigh
That thy path is all forlorn
    With no lover's whisper nigh.

Will it then suffice to know,
   Though no love disturb thy rest,
That the passing strangers show
   An unusual interest?

'None,' they say, 'of common men
   May that lady's lover be;'
If thou hear their whisper then,
   Will it be enough for thee?

‹

AT HER DOOR

A FOOL for my doubting and dreaming,
  And following up and down !
Shall I fill my life with scheming
  For a touch of my lady's gown ?

Shall I lose the good hours of morning
  For a glance of a careless eye,
And take the wage of scorning,
  And wear shame's livery ?

O footman, O wonder of whiteness
  And diplomatic cockade,
O footman of much politeness
  For my lady's lady's maid,—

As you open the door of her carriage,
  Just tell her I've gone away,
But will come to dance at her marriage
  On somebody's happy day.

LOVE IN SPRING

SHE is fair and she is young,
   As so many a maid has been,
As so many a bard has sung
   When in Spring the world was green :
     Ah, how oft have poets sung
     That a girl was fair and young!
      Shall I then sing?
        No, no, no,
     Love's a silly thing,
And comes and goes with Spring.

She is young and she is fair—
   Many a maid is fair as she ;
She has coils of yellow hair—
   Men have painted cunningly
     Brighter hair in Venice old,
     Hair that drained the sun for gold.
      Shall I then try?
        No, I tell thee, no,
     Love's a summer sigh
And gone ere swallows fly.

She is fair ; I cannot tell
  Why I muse on such a thing,
Read her frolic face so well,
  And singing swear I will not sing :
    Fain would I, as others may,
    Smile to see her pass my way,
      And careless sing—
        Tra la la,
      Love's a silly thing
And mars the merry Spring.

E

ON A WESTERN RIVER

I DREAM a dream of a western land
  And a flowing river, and borne along,
With a wall of trees on either hand,
  I lean my ear to their murmured song ;
And my heart is at rest on that river fair,
For never a thought of love is there.

The stream is full as my heart of peace,
  The wind is soft as a mother's kiss,
And wonder and doubt and trouble cease,
  And my heart is at rest, and the cause is this—
That the forest is filled with music rare,
But never a note of love is there.

The moon rides out in the sky at night,
  And the river runs silver all down to the sea,
And the deep dark woods for my deep delight
  Breathe odours of unseen flower and tree ;
And I float and I dream, and in dream I know
That Love lies drowned in the stream below.

His white limbs stir on their gravelled bed,
  As the heart of the river were beating there ;
Dark down by the rushes the comely head,
  And dank are the curls of the sunbright hair ;
And cold smooth fishes, where dead Love lies,
Pass on with round unheeding eyes.

HALF-HEARTED

IF I could love thee, love, a little more,
  If on no April day thy love would fail,
If in my golden field were all thy store,
  And all my joy within thy garden pale—
Then would I teach my heart to be full fond
For ever, and a little bit beyond.

If Spring anemone were not so frail,
  If all the summer long sweet rose were gay,
If I were true as Arthur in the tale,
  And thou could'st love like Juliet in the play—
Then would I teach my heart to be full fond
For ever, and a little bit beyond.

But as, meseems, I am but wayward-true,
  And wayward-false, fair love, thou seem'st to be,
As I some day must sigh for something new,
  And thou each day for life's monotony,
Turn thine eyes from me ere we grow too fond,
And let me pass a little bit beyond.

A MOMENT

Down from my window I lean and look ;
　The road is all full of sunlight sweet ;
Below me a bird flies fast and afar,
　And his shadow flies on the sunlit street.

And is it love in my heart, I pray,
　Or the shadow of love from some tender book ?
Well, be it love or the shadow of love,
　It passes away as I lean and look.

LOVE AND THE LITTLE MERCHANT

\

YOUNG Love has a shirt of the woven flame
   That clings and burns on the breast,
Till the heart of the wearer is faint with shame
   And his wild eyes ache for rest.

And I have been slave of this fierce boy Love,
   And careless of work and gain,
For I held no joy in the world above
   The throb and the lull of the pain.

But now I have bound him, hands and eyes,
   And shipped him across the seas
As a bale of remarkable merchandise
   For inquisitive Japanese.

And lord of myself and lord of mirth,
   I sing through the working day,
For joy that beauty remains on the earth,
   And that Love has been packed away.

A SONG FOR GALATEA

HARK! Is it sound or silence? The wide sea
Is breathless calm, and yet a whisper breathed
And died i' the breathing—is it sound or no?
The air is all expectant. See, what light
Breaks with the foam afar, with quickening air
Laughter and music! Hither apace they drive,
Riot of Nymph and Triton, strange sea-beast,
Foam flashed and shaken jewels. Throned o'er all,
Fenced from rude sport, yet tuned for merry play,
Rides Galatea, fairest maid that charms
The wild-eyed sea-birds 'twixt the sea and sky.
  Galatea, here to thee,
  Queen of mirth and jollity,
  Loud we raise our jocund song,
  Shouting with thy triton throng,
  Shouting as their horns outring
  For the pleasant song we sing,

Singing loud and clear to thee,
Queen of mirth and jollity.

Aye, perchance, on yonder shore
Acis leads his flock once more,
Stands and stares across the wave,
Hopeful of thy pageant brave ;
Aye, perchance, or Polypheme,
Where the mountain torrents stream,
Slow to think, and slow to move,
Slowly feels the tides of love
Rising through his monstrous frame,
Till his huge lips shape thy name,
Galatea, hailing thee
Queen of mirth and jollity.

When young Raphael did stand
Lone on Adriatic strand,
Peering out across the brine,
What saw he save charms of thine ?
Turned he from the Virgin's face,
From her sweet religious grace,
From the chamber tapestried,
From the cloister turned aside,
Turned as bridegroom to his bride,

And, afire with sea-king's mood,
Laughed in glory where he stood,
Calling loud across the sea :
' Galatea, fair and free,
Let me witch the world with thee ! '

I, meseems, am Acis now
For one moment's joy, as thou,
Tossing all thy tresses free
To the wild wind's revelry,
Lookest with thy sea-blue eyes
Deep to mine.   Before me rise
Pomps and pageants pure and bright,
Meet for Raphael's delight
When he passed from cloister dim,
Saw thee all in sunlight swim,
And so gave his heart to thee,
Queen of light and liberty.

Queen, let me thy pageant greet,
Let me plunge to kiss thy feet,
And amid thy jocund throng
Wind the shell or shout the song,
Riding where the leaping waves,
High above thy cool green caves,

Toss their flying crests in glee,
And the brave breeze fitfully
Brings the goodly smell of brine.
Galatea, make me thine,
Least of all who sing for thee,
Queen of light and liberty!

A GIRL TO HER GLASS

LITTLE face so near, so near,
   Laughing lips and eyes that shine,
Can it be, my dearest dear,
   All those pretty looks are mine ?

Laughing eyes, be not too bold,
   If a man should praise your blue ;
Men have said, as I've been told,
   Many a thing that was not true.

When the sky is clear above,
   And the earth is green below,
Better laughter is than love—
   Love may come or love may go.

Little lambs are in the grass,
   Little fleeces in the sky ;
Everything, where Spring doth pass,
   Pretty is—and so am I.

SO IS THE STORY TOLD

A FAIR head meekly bowed
  With shy glance after ;
Voices not over-loud,
  And a low sweet laughter :
So is the story told,
Up in the cottage old,
  Under the smoky rafter.

A pale girl flushed to red
  By quick new feeling,
Yet slow to bend the head
  For lover's kneeling :
So is the story told,
Down 'mid the white and gold,
  Under the painted ceiling.

THISBE

SHE lives in the smoky city,
   Low down by the railway line ;
But she asks for no man's pity,
   Nor cares for verse of mine.

All day she's hither and thither,
   And often her work is hard ;
But sometimes in fine weather
   She rests a bit in the yard.

With her mop and pail behind her,
   She leans her arms on the wall,
And hopes that there he'll find her,
   Her lover strong and tall.

High in the air above her
   The great trains outward go,
And many a lass and her lover
   May journey to Jericho.

But when from the neighbour doorway
    He comes and leans on the wall,
The world would be in a poor way
    If that were not best of all.

È MORTO

A PAINTER painted Death with languid eyes
   Rose-lipped and sweeter than a living maid,
All laid along with Spring anemones,
   And with the ambushed violet low laid ;
And by her side a shadowed stream did flow,
And made mute music on the canvas. 'Oh,'
The painter sighed, 'to lie by that dear head !'
He sighed for pictured death and found instead
Death. He is dead.

WINGED JOY

A PAINTER painted life at a window toward the
    sea ;
Live birds flew into the room and chirped as glad
    as he.
O life, life, life, the soul is winged as a bird ;
There is angel and singing lark, but where is a
    third
If the soul of the artist be not a wingèd thing,
To sing i' the dawn, at noon, and at golden eve to
    sing ?
'Give me thine heart,' said the man, 'O bird that
    soarest free ! '
'Open thy heart,' said the bird, 'and make it a
    nest for me.'

A SONG OF PROSERPINE

HER eyes were lights of the morning,
  Her song of the meadows gay,
But the dark man at eventide
  Had stolen her away—

Away from the sunbright upland,
  Where the folded sheep are fed,
Away from her father's cottage door,
  Away from her childhood's bed.

And ah, if her mother could see her
  Who once was glad of her birth,
And hear her laugh in the gaslight glare
  A laugh of little mirth.

AFTER RAIN

THE rain was all golden at even
  When the sun rode out on the air,
A gift and a glory of heaven
  For travelling folk to share.

The surly muttering thunder
  Had threatened and passed away,
Dull clouds had been rolled from under
  The feet of the passing day.

Our road was as silver before us,
  Our hedges alight with gems ;
The soft blue sky high o'er us
  Was swept by the angel hems.

And we were too glad for playing,
  And we were too sad for tears,
But only our hearts were praying,
  As they prayed in childhood's years.

And angels of ancient story
  Came forth in ranks untold,
Till the gates of the western glory
  Were thronged with the spears of gold.

And far on the airs of even
  Came shout and armour-clang,
And deep in the deeps of heaven
  An angel trumpet rang.

TO THE LADY PORTIA THESE

QUICK from fog and frost away,
Fly, my song, with greeting gay
To fair Belmont's lady fair;
Up, my song, to purer air,
Up, as lark doth heavenward spring;
Quick, as swallow dips his wing,
Slanting to the summer sea;
Quick, away with frolic glee,
Humble greeting, greeting gay
To the lady Portia!

Fair she is, and passing wise;
She has shapen destinies;
Learning ever, wise to teach,
Swift of tongue, and true of speech,
Wise in counsel, firm in deed,
Helper in man's utmost need,
Brave as wise, and true as brave,
Quick to feel, and strong to save.

Fly, my song, and humbly pay
Honour to great Portia!

Brave she is, and sweet withal,
Queen at life's high festival,
Queen of laughter, keen of wit,
Quick to aim and sure to hit,
Laughing light and laughing ever
At the foolish jest or clever,
Laughing first and jesting after,
For she scarce can speak for laughter
Who men's endless folly sees,
Antics, inconsistencies ;
Wiser than all men, more gay
Than a child is Portia.

Bright on Adriatic sea
Plays the sunlight laughingly ;
Soft on Belmont's lawns by night
Flows and spreads the fair moonlight ;
Countless years has Venice stood
Steadfast on the shifting flood.
Steadfast heart, unswerving will,
Noble purpose, matchless skill,

Tenderness of moon's soft ray,
Splendour of Venetian day
Or of Venus' jocund birth,
Naught of malice, all of mirth,
Laughter, learning, love, and play,
All good things are Portia.

Hie then song, with favouring wind,
And a happy journey find,
And, when thou art o'er the trees
Of fair Belmont's terraces,
Bow thee to thy lady's knife!
Kiss the hand that takes thy life;
Take one kiss and breathe one sigh
When she cuts thy cord, and lie
In her hand beneath her smile.
She will laugh a little while—
For she laughs at little things;
Then perchance she'll fold thy wings,
And so lay thee on her heart:
Then, my song, how blest thou art,
On the home of trust and play,
On the heart of Portia!

THE COAST OF KENT

THE breeze, that stayed to pipe and trill
In wires that climb the highway hill,
The fluting breeze flies fair and free
To frolic with the ships at sea,
And sunstruck like a mirror bright
The chalk cliffs leap to sudden light.

A SONG OF EARTH

High in the air the skylarks swing,
Like poet's swift imagining,
And, while the tremulous air prolongs
The lilt and rapture of their songs,
The glorious sun in spendthrift mood
Pours far and wide his golden flood,
Till lost in light those small birds be
Notes of one harmony.

The open downs spread free and far
To where the plains of ocean are ;
Seaward the fisher boats outspring
To take the sunshine on their wing ;
Seaward and free the following breeze
From play amid the inland trees
Leaps like a joy, and wavelets run
To meet the sun.

Low 'neath the grass the gray-coat mole
  Pushes a soft and silent way
To the unseen goal ;
  But e'en beneath his coat of gray
That digging friar's heart will sing
    In praise of Spring.

White clouds that fleck the blue,
White sails unfurled,
Spring comes anew
To the new world,
And high in air and 'neath the sod
The joy of God.

PRINTED BY
SPOTTISWOODE AND CO., NEW-STREET SQUARE
LONDON

.

www.ingramcontent.com/pod-product-compliance
Lightning Source LLC
Chambersburg PA
CBHW031453270326
41930CB00007B/973